On The Far Side Of Poplar Pond

Written by:
Anjanette Walchshauser

Illustrated by:
Paul Miller

WestBow Press books may be ordered through booksellers or by contacting:

WestBow Press
A Division of Thomas Nelson & Zondervan
1663 Liberty Drive
Bloomington, IN 47403
www.westbowpress.com
1 (866) 928-1240

ISBN: 978-1-4908-9177-4 (sc)
ISBN: 978-1-4908-9178-1 (e)

Print information available on the last page.

WestBow Press rev. date: 08/26/2015

"For my children and the wonderful and creative way God brought them into my life. For my husband, the best friend I could ever imagine. For my parents, who believe in me. And most importantly for the glory of my God!"

– A.W.

"For my beautiful family, I love you."

– P.M.

On the far side of Poplar Pond, a
turtle looked up to the moon.

She asked God for help really soon, for her baby girl needed a home. The mama turtle trusted that God had a plan. She couldn't provide the home her baby turtle needed, for the mama turtle was all alone.

Dude Duck splashed, and he swam. He splashed, and he swam, diving down, diving down,
diving
down,
down,
d
o
w
n ...

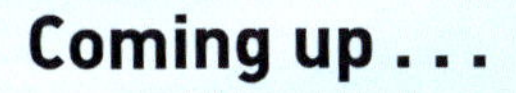

SPLASH!!!

Mama Duck and Daddy Duck cheered for him. “Hooray, Son!” They had quite a laugh. But in their hearts, they prayed that God would bring them another child to share their home.

Across the pond came Old Owl
soaring with his wings so wide.

He gently landed right by
Daddy Duck's side.

"We have a girl for you," Old Owl said. "She needs a family, she needs a nest, and she needs some love and care. She needs someone who will love her best."

Mama Duck cried tears of joy. Daddy Duck sang, "God has answered our prayers."

Tina Turtle was her name, and she was tiny and pink. They took her home and prepared a place in the nest she would forever call her own.

A young brown mouse watched from the field, amazed at what he saw. "Old Owl, Old Owl!" he called. "Why did you bring the ducks that turtle?"

"The ducks have been praying that God would give them an opportunity to share their love with another child," answered the wise Old Owl.

"And He did."

"But you can't just bring a baby turtle to another family. It just doesn't seem right," stammered the young mouse.

"It is called adoption." explained Old Owl.

"A whation?" The mouse was confused.

The wise Old Owl slowly explained to the young mouse, "Sometimes a child is born, and the birth mother cannot give the child *all* that the child needs. Sometimes the best way she can show her *love* is to place the child in a new home where he or she will be safe, loved, and celebrated for all that the child is! That child becomes a part of the new family *forever*. That is called adoption!"

"But ...," the young mouse paused. "They don't look the same!"

"Oh, young mouse," began Old Owl, "is looking like your mama or daddy what makes them special to you? Is that what makes you feel love? Is having the same color eyes what makes you feel safe?"

The mouse shook his head.

"Of course not," laughed Old Owl. "It is the kisses when you fall down, the stories at bedtime, the hugs when you are sad, and your parents just being there when you wake up day after day after day that makes you feel special!"

"The Duck family will be that family for the young turtle, just like your family is that for you!"

"Who came up with that idea?" wondered the mouse.

"God did," replied Old Owl.

"Once we believe in Him and His son, Jesus, as our Savior, He adopts us too. He gives us everything He has, and we are forever a part of His family."

As Tina grew, she always knew that she was right at home. That God has made a plan for her to be loved, to be kissed, to be cuddled by her forever family. . .

She splashed, and she swam. She splashed, and she swam right next to Dude,

diving down, diving down
diving down,
down,
d
o
w
n.

Mama and Daddy cheered for them, "Hooray, Son! Hooray, Daughter!"

They had quite a laugh.

Every night when the moon was high, Mama and Daddy spoke to God, who provided it all. It sometimes made Mama cry, her heart full of joy, as Daddy would try to find the words to say thank you to God for putting their family together in the way that was best of all!

And on the far side of Poplar Pond,
a turtle would often look up,
and with a heart full of love,
thank God for the help He sent her
way. She knew in her heart every day
that her baby girl had a home.

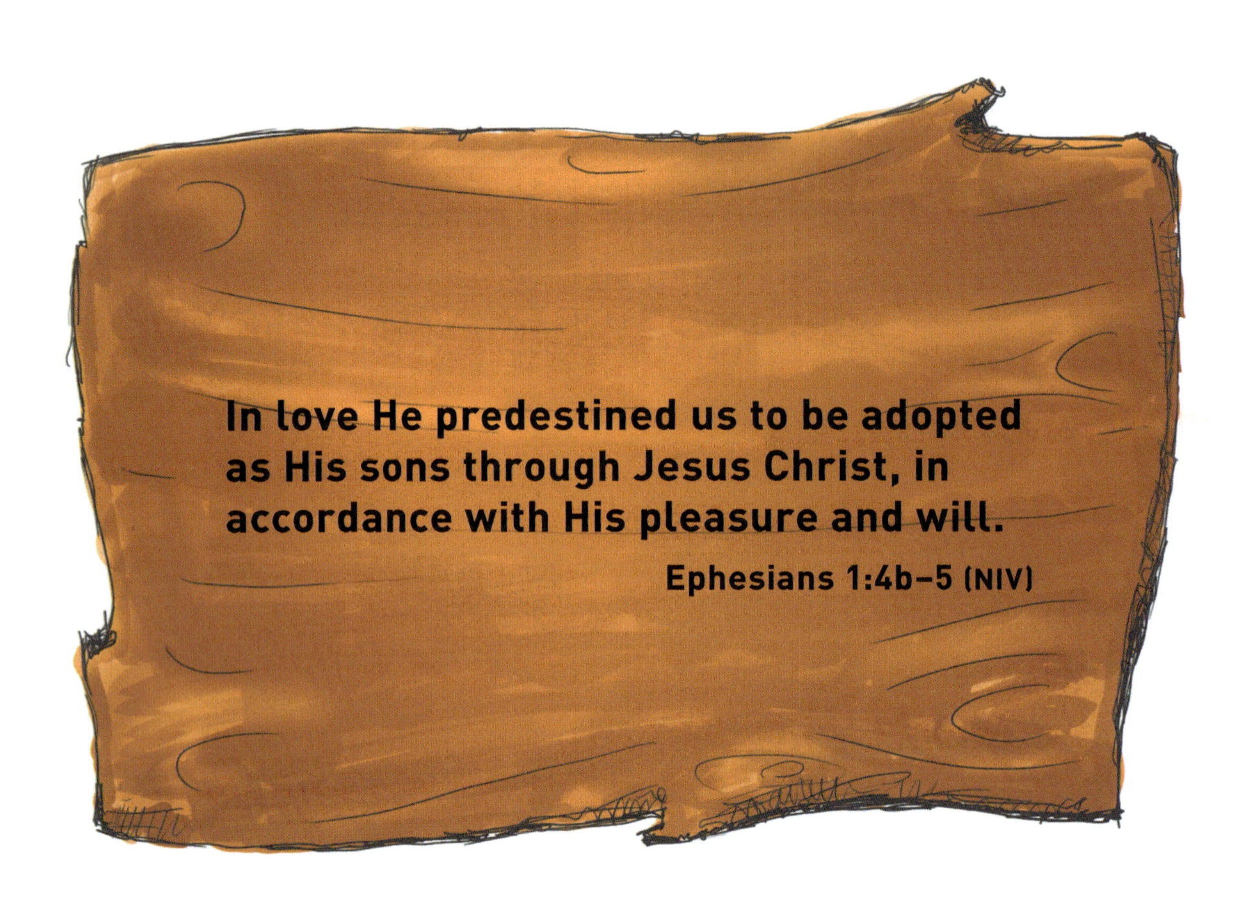

In love He predestined us to be adopted as His sons through Jesus Christ, in accordance with His pleasure and will.

Ephesians 1:4b–5 (NIV)

CPSIA information can be obtained
at www.ICGtesting.com
Printed in the USA
LVIC04n1915231215
467620LV00008B/84

* 9 7 8 1 4 9 0 8 9 1 7 7 4 *